Black Collectibles

Mammy and Her Friends

Jackie Young
Photographs Thomas North

1469 Morstein Road, West Chester, Pennsylvania 19380

Large, metal, Aunt Jemima breakfast club pin was given away free at pancake promotions. These have been reproduced. Circa 1953. (4″ across)

Front cover photo: Old, painted, metal, mammy doorstop and bank. (9″ & 5½″)

Title page photo: Original Luzianne coffee mammy salt and pepper shakers of molded green plastic were a promotional set made by F&F Mold & Die Works of Dayton, Ohio. Marked F&F. Circa 1950-1951. (5¼″)

Copyright © 1988 by Jackie Young.
Library of Congress Catalog Number: 88-62979.
Printed in the United States of America.
ISBN: 0-88740-149-X
Published by Schiffer Publishing Ltd.
1469 Morstein Road, West Chester
Pennsylvania 19380
This book may be purchased from the publisher.
Please include $2.00 postage.
Try your bookstore first.

This book is dedicated to:

Jill Pence

Janis Knowles

&

Ann Davenport

Beautiful 1955 Aunt Jemima pancake magazine advertisement
featuring characters from the made-up Aunt Jemima legend.

ACKNOWLEDGMENTS

To all those who were involved in the making of this book, I owe profound thanks:

Ken Anthony; Pauline de Morcia; Gene Galloway; Beth & Nick Garrett; Justin Jones; Wayne Jordan; Bonnie Kidd; Janis Knowles; Anita Luquette; Mel Mitchell; Jacquelyne North; Jill Pence; Kathy Ratcliffe; Gail Sargent; Lynda & Richard Saxton; Scott L. Shafer; Nark Sitrin; Dwayne Teal; Alice Timmerman; Gloria Young; Jimmy & Tom Zinn; Wellsville Carnegie Public Library; Dallas Public Library; Quicksilver Photo Lab; and Competitive Camera

Matching pair of ceramic cookie jars called 'Mammy' and 'Cooky' were probably made by the Pioneer Pottery Company of Ohio for the Pearl China Co. Marked-Pearl China Co., hand decorated, 22 KT Gold, U.S.A. Circa 1940's. (10¼" & 10½")

FOREWORD

I became a devotee of mammy collectibles because of the warm, happy memories I associate with them. Growing up in the 1950's, I can remember many pleasant times spent in kitchens, including my grandmothers, decorated with the friendly, smiling, motherly black mammy image.

It was only later, during my teenage years, that I came to realize that the black items I saw had a darker side to them. They were stereotypes and caricatures that helped reinforce ignorant white notions of racial superiority. That most of the objects drove home the belittling idea that most black people were only fit for

Kitchen and table size salt and pepper shakers named salty and peppy were distributed by the Pearl China Co. Marked Pearl China Co. Hand-decorated, 22 kt. gold, U.S.A. Circa 1940's. (4½" & 7½")

Four piece brown glazed, red clay measuring cup set. They look like clown faces with big round noses. Marked-Des.Pat.Pend., paper label-Thames Handpainted Japan. Circa 1950's. (1½"-3")

menial jobs like cooks, waiters, or servants. Thank goodness the civil rights movement ended this once common portrayal of an entire race and closed that chapter in American culture.

The field of black memorabilia collecting is one that can last a lifetime. The areas that a collection can span include such diverse fields as kitchen collectibles, advertisements, figurines, calendars, packages, souvenirs, novelties, toys, linens, photographica, books, etc. The list is almost endless. By collecting black memorabilia you can have the dual pleasure of decorating your home and investing in objects that will almost certainly increase in monetary value as time goes by.

The Aunt Jemima Story

The pretty city of St. Louis, Missouri was the original birthplace of Aunt Jemima pancakes. In 1889 a smart newspaperman named Chris L. Rutt was inspired with the idea of inventing a self-raising pancake mix. Rutt named the resulting pancake mix after a catchy cakewalk song. He had heard it sung by the vaudeville team of Baker and Farrell that had performed in St. Joseph that fall. The melodious tune was called "Aunt Jemima."

The R.T. Davis Milling Co., also of St. Joseph, bought the business from Rutt a few years later. At the 1893 Columbian Exposition in Chicago, the new owners launched Aunt Jemima pancake mix to fame

Two piece Aunt Jemima cardboard puzzle, needs string. On the back of one mammy is printed "It will puzzle you to separate these two cards without untying the string. But it will not puzzle you to decide which is the best pancake flour." Circa 1902-1916. (4")

Old Davis Milling Co. magazine advertisement for Aunt Jemima's Pancake Flour. It featured an imported Climbing Aunt Jemima doll for 10 cents and one package coupon, and rag doll family ready to cut and stuff, for 16 cents and four coupons. Circa 1905.

Small, metal, Aunt Jemima pancake club pin was made by Adcraft Mfg. Co. of Chicago. Circa 1953. (2¼")

Left: A 1949 Aunt Jemima magazine advertisement featuring the rag doll family.

Right: A 1951 Aunt Jemima magazine advertisement with a cookie jar offer.

with an immensely popular display booth located in the agricultural hall. The company, to reinforce the brand image, hired a black cook from Kentucky named Nancy Green to play the part of Aunt Jemima. She demonstrated how to mix the pancakes and cooked over one million at the fair. Until her death in 1923, Green traveled the country as Aunt Jemima promoting the Davis Milling Co.'s pancake mix.

When Davis Milling Co. hired Nancy Green they also made up a legend to fit the fictional Aunt Jemima persona. Aunt Jemima, they claimed, was a simple, earnest, smiling mammy cook who was a slave on Colonel Higbee's plantation in the State of Louisiana. She was supposed to be famous throughout the South for her delicious, secret pancake recipe. Twenty years after the Civil War, a persuasive representative of the Davis Milling Co. bought from Aunt Jemima her famous recipe and talked her into directing its preparation at the Davis Mills. This fanciful legend was used for decades, until the 1960's, to promote Aunt Jemima pancakes.

In 1925 the Davis Milling Co. sold the pancake recipe and the Aunt Jemima name to the Quaker Oats Co., a division of the American Cereal Co.

The warm, smiling face that most people today associate with Aunt Jemima is that of Edith Wilson. In the 1950's Quaker Oats hired Edith to play the role of Aunt Jemima in advertisements, commercials, and personal appearances. Edith Wilson was born in 1897 and recorded her first record in 1921. She had a regular part in the "Amos and Andy" show on both radio and television. Her most famous movie was "To Have and Have Not" starring Humphrey Bogart. Edith is best remembered by the general public for becoming Aunt Jemima, which she played for over 18 years.

In 1950 the copper-plated Aunt Jemima spice shelf was replaced with a less expensive plastic shelf. The plastic shelf came in red or white. (12" x 2")

An Aunt Jemima six piece spice set in red plastic including jars for allspice, ginger, cloves, cinnamon, nutmeg, and paprika became available for purchase with coupon in 1949. A copper-plated spice shelf decorated with a steamboat scene and a turned-up, scalloped edge were also offered. The shelf was only sold in 1949. (jars 4", shelf 12" x 4 ¼")

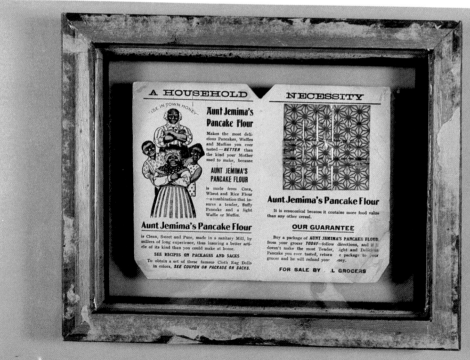

Front and back view of Davis Milling Co. Aunt Jemima cardboard needlebook. Circa 1905. (2-¾")

Aunt Jemima yellow plastic sugar with lid and Uncle Mose creamers were sold through a boxtop coupon offer. Marked F&F. Circa 1949. (2¼" & 2½")

Red plastic Luzianne coffee mammy salt and pepper made by F&F. After F&F Mold & Die Works sold the mold, the later versions made had the F&F symbol marked out. Circa 1960's.

A December 1916 Davis Milling Co. Aunt Jemima magazine advertisement featuring a rag doll family for 3 boxtops and 10 cents in stamps or coins. Notice the difference between this rag doll family and the one shown in the earlier ad. (10" x 13")

The first box top coupon offer by Aunt Jemima were salt and pepper shakers in two sizes for the kitchen and table. They were made of molded plastic and had spray painted trim. The F&F Mold and Die Company of Dayton, Ohio manufactured them for Aunt Jemima. Marked-F&F. Circa 1948. (3½" & 5¼")

Aunt Jemima corn meal mix lighters made by Scripto in the U.S.A. were given away by Quaker Oats salesman. An Aunt Jemima pancake mix lighter was also given out. Circa 1955. (2½")

A March 1921 magazine advertisement for Aunt Jemima pancake flour featuring the realistic mammy redrawn in 1917.

Quaker Oats mug in the shape of their well-known Quaker man symbol was a coupon offer. It was made by F&F Mold and Die Co. of Dayton, Ohio. Marked-F&F. Circa 1953. (3½")

It seemed that everybody wanted to taste those golden-brown cakes

At the World's Fair in '93 *Aunt Jemima* was a sensation

"I's in town, Honey!"

AUNT JEMIMA PANCAKE FLOUR

How to get the Funny Rag Dolls

Aunt Jemima
SELF-RISING
WHITE
CORN MEAL
MIX

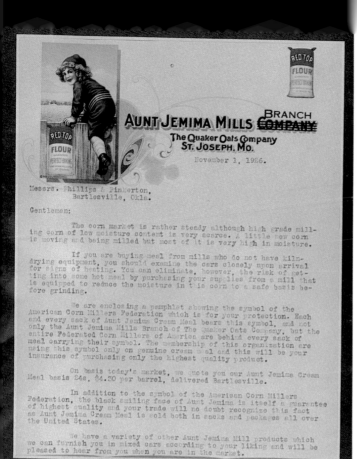

One of a kind letter on original Quaker Oats' Aunt Jemima mills stationery is dated Nov. 1, 1926.

Aunt Jemima rag doll family after purchaser stuffed with cotton or rags. The stuffed versions are not as valuable as the unstuffed dolls. Circa 1949.

A January 1929 magazine advertisement for Quaker Oats' Aunt Jemima Buckwheat flour. Davis Milling Co. sold Aunt Jemima to Quaker Oats in 1925.

Aunt Jemima plastic rag doll family, which came already cut and sealed, included Aunt Jemima, Uncle Mose, Diana, and Wade. The whole set cost 75 cents and three boxtops. Circa 1949. (12¾" & 8¾")

Rare cardboard Halloween mask in the shape of Aunt Jemima with more advertising on the back. Circa 1905-1916. (10½")

The plastic Aunt Jemima syrup pitcher originally started as a boxtop coupon offer. To spur sales against the then top selling Pillsbury pancake mix, the company began giving them away free to customers by attaching them to boxes of pancake mix. This promotion made Aunt Jemima leader of the pancake mixes. Marked-F&F. Circa 1949. (5½")

The last cookie jar boxtop coupon offer made by Aunt Jemima was this soft molded red plastic model. The public did not respond well to the offer. Hard to find. No marks. Circa early 1950's. (10¼")

Plastic Aunt Jemima cookie jars were a boxtop coupon offer. The faces came in two colors, brown and black. The black face cookie jar was first offered in 1948 and the brown face cookie jar in 1949. The cookie jar was offered by coupon promotion through-1951. The brown face is harder to find. Marked-F&F. (11½")

In 1950 Aunt Jemima offered the creamer and sugar in green and blue plastic by boxtop coupon. Only short runs of these colors were made. The public rejected them because they didn't match the other Aunt Jemima coupon items. Hard to find. Circa 1950. (2¼" & 2½")

The paper recipe book *Tempting New Aunt Jemima Pancake 'n Waffle Recipes* has a pleasant white and blue cover. Circa 1950's. (4" x 6")

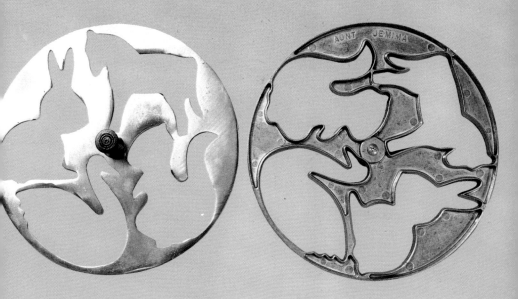

A hard-to-find Aunt Jemima mail-in premium is this metal cut-out animal pancake mold. The animals included a swan, squirrel, horse, and rabbit. Circa 1950. (8½" across)

Portable pancake grill, model R-601, used by the Quaker Oats Co. to demonstrate how to make Aunt Jemima pancakes to the public at stores, county fairs, etc. After the pancakes were made, they were served on paper plates decorated with a picture of Aunt Jemima. The yellow plastic pancake shaker attached to the side is also marked Aunt Jemima. It also came in green and red plastic. Stove circa 1948, pancake shaker circa 1948.

Aunt Jemima complete recipe cardset. The set contained sixteen different recipes from famous eating places pictured on the front of each card. An Aunt Jemima recipe box marked 'Aunt Jemima' was also available. Circa 1949.

Cardboard sewing kit in the shape of a Luzianne coffee can was a promotional item. The set included a needle threader and two packages of needles. (4½")

Colorful cardboard box used to hold Fun-to-Wash brand washing powder manufactured by Hygienic Laboratories of Buffalo, N.Y. Circa 1930's. (3¼")

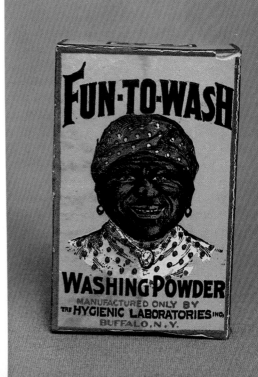

The paper recipe book called *Aunt Jemima's New Temptilatin' Menus and Recipes* has a picture of Aunt Jemima holding a plate of pancakes on the cover. Circa 1950. (4" x 6")

The ceramic cookie jar 'Sambo the Chef' was advertised by Sears in 1942 and sold for $1.19. It was made in the U.S.A. In 1941 the same jar was advertised by Sears as a Japanese import and sold for 98 cents. The mammy and chef cookie jars shown were both distributed by the National Silver Company of New York, a selling agency for several potteries. Both marked - N.S.C.O., U.S.A. Circa early 1940's. (9½" & 9")

Paper Aunt Jemima *New Temptilatin Recipes* book has a red and white gingham cover. Circa 1948. (4" x 6")

Plaid mammy creamer and sugar were featured in a 1940 wholesale catalog. They are made of hand-painted ceramic. Marked-Japan. Circa late 1930's-1941. (4" & 3")

A 1949 Aunt Jemima Pancake magazine advertisement with a spice set offer.

Rare, hand-painted, ceramic butter dish in the plaid mammy finish. Marked-Japan. Circa late 1930's-1941. (4")

A heart-shaped cake decorates the cover of the paper recipe book *Aunt Jemima Cake Mix Miracles*. Circa 1953. (4½" x 6½")

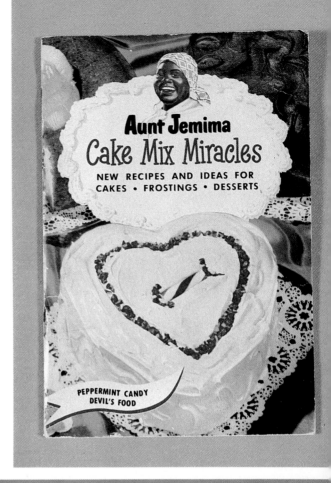

Orange, blue, and green plaid mammy ceramic salt and pepper shakers were made in Japan. Marked-Japan. Circa late 1930's-1941. (5")

Four pound coffee tin with handle used for Mammy's favorite brand coffee. (10¾")

Cute, ceramic, plaid mammy planter has a yellow and white basketweave design plant holder in the back. Marked-Japan. Circa late 1930's-1941. (5½")

Three pound tin coffee can with handle used for Luzianne coffee. Circa 1940's-early 1950's. (7¼")

Brown, fired ceramic, laughing mammy cookie jar with the lid in the front is decorated with white and red painting. No marks. Circa 1960's. (8")

Heavy creamy yellow and brown smiling mammy cookie jar made of high gloss pottery was manufactured by the Mosaic Tile Co. of Zanesville, Ohio. The jar was also in blue. The design for the jar received a U.S. design patent in 1944. (12½")

Three-piece set consisting of a mammy salt, cook pepper, and stove-shaped sugar bowl can be found in green, yellow, blue and pink ceramic with gold trim. Attributed U.S.A. Circa 1950s. (4¾", 5", 4¾")

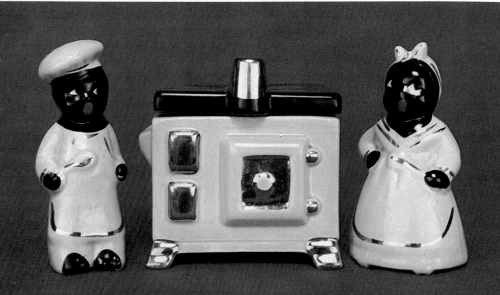

Hard-to-find mammy cookie jar of cold painted, fired ceramic was made in Japan. Circa mid-1940's to early 1950's. (9")

Salt and pepper set shaped like two young black children playing in a basket is in excellent condition. Sticker marked-Betson's, Handpainted, Japan. Circa 1950's. (basket 4", shakers 3¾")

Cute, wide-eyed, young mammy holding a spoon is a ceramic cookie jar. The original cold paint shows wear. No marks. Circa late 1940's-early 1950's. (10")

McCoy mammy ceramic cookie jar dressed in white with green trim and wearing a red headscarf has the word "cookies" across the front of her skirt. Marked-McCoy. Circa 1940's. (10½")

Pretty ceramic cookie jar in the shape of a mammy carrying a basket of flowers was manufactured by Abingdon Potteries in Abingdon, Illinois. Abingdon produced decorative items including cookie jars between 1934 to 1950. This jar can be found with different decoration. Marked-Abingdon U.S.A. (9¼")

Plaid mammy ceramic matchholder is hard to find. Marked-Japan. Circa late 1930's-1941. 5¾")

Red clay with brown glaze three-piece set including salt, pepper, and sugar bowl is decorated with purple hairbows and white chef hat. The set can be found marked either Japan or Occupied Japan. Circa 1945-1952. (3", 5", 3")

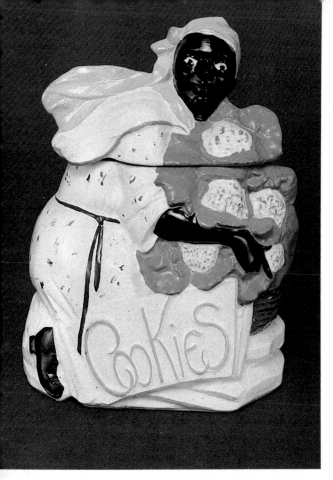

A rare cookie jar by McCoy pottery of Roseville, Ohio is called *Mammy with Cauliflower*. The cold painting on this jar has been retouched. Marked McCoy U.S.A. Circa 1939.

Tray with attached mammy figurine holds three barrel-shaped containers marked pepper, mustard, and salt. Circa 1940's. (5½")

National Silver Company
mammy cookie jar can be
found with varied cold
painted decorative detail.
Marked-N.S.C.O., U.S.A.
Circa early 1940's. (9")

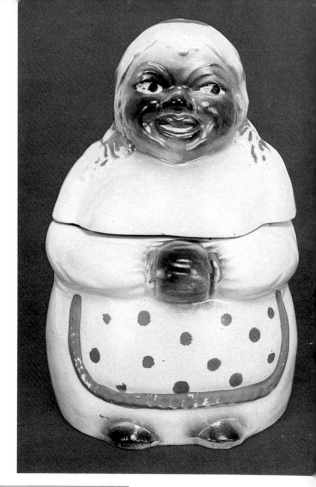

Oil and vinegar set shaped
like a cook and mammy.
Each is holding a spoon.
Marked-Japan. Circa
1950's. (5⅛")

Two pair of small painted chalkware salt and pepper shakers. Chalkware sets, especially in good condition, are hard to find. Circa 1940's. (2¾", 2⅞")

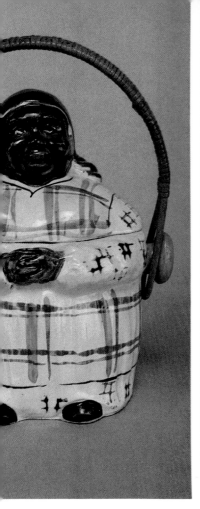

The plaid mammy cracker or bisquit jars with woven wicker handles came in two sizes and were imported to the U.S.A. from Japan. The hand-painted decorative finish can vary widely. The mate to these jars, a black butler, was pictured in a 1940 wholesale catalog. All marked-Japan. Circa late 1930's to 1941. (8", 8", 10")

Aunt Jemima metal advertising button. The slogan "I'se in town honey" was trademarked by the Davis Milling Co. in 1912. The company claimed the use of the slogan from 1905. The company dropped the mammy caricature in 1916. (⅞")

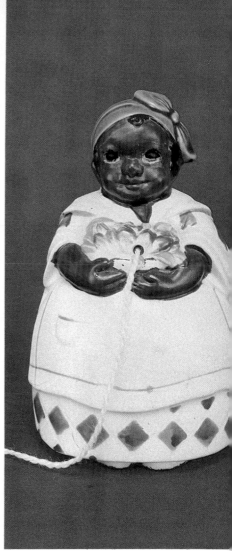

Metlox Potteries of California introduced this charming cookie jar shaped like a mammy stirring a bowl in January of 1987. It is still being manufactured and also comes in yellow. Marked-Metlox Calif. U.S.A. (13")

Adorable, well-detailed stringholder of ceramic is shaped like a young mammy holding a bunch of flowers. Marked-Japan, Fred Hirode. Circa 1940's. (6¾")

Small smiling black chef cookie or cracker jar with his hands in his pockets is wearing blue and white striped trousers. Marked-Japan. Circa 1940's-1950's. (8¼")

Two different pair of dark brown glazed ceramic mammy and cook shakers. Both marked-Japan. (4" & 4¾")

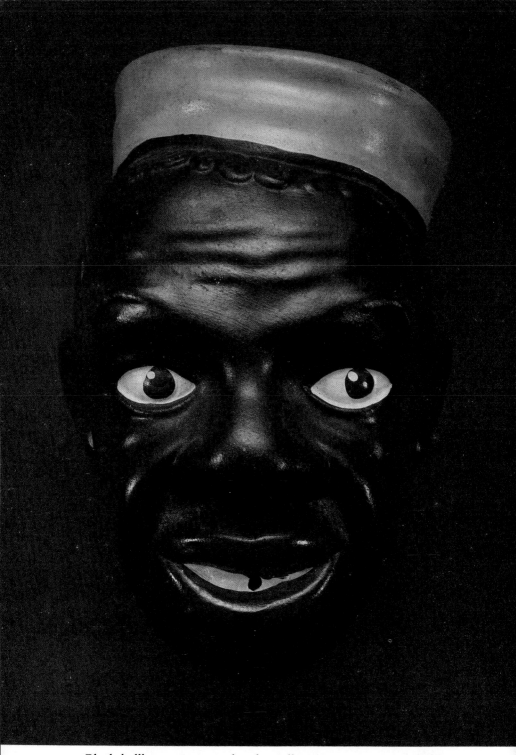

Black bellboy wearing a bright yellow cap was a stringholder made by Fredericksburg Art Pottery in Fredericksburg, Ohio. Marked-Fredericksburg Art Pottery U.S.A. Circa 1939-1949. (6½")

Very popular plaid mammy string holder was featured in a 1940
wholesale catalog. Marked-Japan. Circa late 1930's-1941. (6½")

Charming, ceramic little girl dressed in white with a look of
surprise on her face is a stringholder. Marked-Japan. (6½")

Two pair of Japanese ceramic shakers shaped like a cook's and
mammy's head. Circa 1st pr.-1940's, 2nd pr.-1950's. (2½", 2¼",
2⅞", 2¼")

Hand-painted ceramic stringholder shaped like a mammy is in excellent condition. Marked-Hand painted Japan. (6¾″)

Colorful ceramic oil and vinegar set with matching salt and pepper shakers were made in Japan. The cruet set has cork-tipped stoppers. Marked-Japan. Circa mid-1940's to mid-1950's. (6″ & 4¾″)

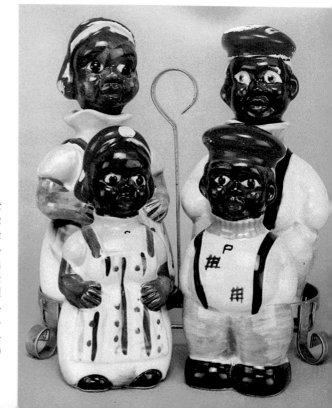

Grinning boy pepper shaker is seated on the toilet-shaped salt shaker. Marked-Japan. Circa mid-1940's to mid-1950's. (4¾")

Exceptional salt and pepper set with beautiful detailing and coloring represent a Valentine couple. Marked-Japan. Circa late 1950's to 1960's. (5")

Salt and pepper set shaped like a seated, nude, black woman with gray hair holding a separate piece of watermelon. The separate head piece nods. Hard to find. Marked-Patent T.T., Swing China, made in Japan. Circa 1930's. (3½")

Ceramic boy dressed in pink and green holding a separate slice of watermelon is a salt and pepper shaker. Marked-Handpainted, Japan. Circa 1950's. (4½")

Mammy statuette dressed in red and yellow is holding a yoke across her shoulders that has a basket-shaped salt and pepper shakers hanging from it. Circa 1940's. (4½")

Large mammy and cook shakers are wearing white aprons decorated with yellow flowers. No marks. Circa early 1950's. (8½" & 8")

Large and small mammy and cook salt and pepper sets. Marked-Relco Japan. Circa 1950's. (5" & 8")

Plaid-dressed mammy and black-coated butler salt and pepper shakers were hand-painted. Marked-Japan. Circa late 1930's to 1941. (6")

Very colorfully painted ceramic mammy and cook shaker set. No marks. (4½")

White ceramic mammy and butler salt and pepper set have brown faces and purple lips. (6″)

Handpainted plaid mammy salt and butler Pepper set. Marked-made in Japan. Circa late 1930's to 1941. (4¾″)

47

Two small sets of Japanese ceramic shakers. One set is shaped like cooks in blue striped trousers, the other set is a cook and mammy. Marked Japan. Circa 1st pr.-1940's, 2nd pr.-1950's. (3¾", 3⅛")

Two small pair of children-shaped shakers. The first pair is a chalkware boy and girl eating watermelon. The second beautifully detailed pair of Japanese ceramic is a boy and girl holding ears of corn. Circa 1st pr.-1940's, 2nd pr.-1950's. (2½" & 3")

Short, fat cook and mammy shakers dressed in white with yellow trim. Marked-Japan. Circa 1945-1952. (2½")

Two small pair of Japanese ceramic shakers. The first set is a mammy and cook dressed in white. The unusual second set is a boy and girl cook holding platters of fruit. Circa late 1940's. (3⅛", 3⅜")

The ceramic smiling cook heads salt and pepper are marked Tehachap. The unmarked mammy and cook shakers have a rich brown glaze. Circa 1st pr.-1940's, 2nd pr.-1950's. (4½", 5¼")

Two sets of handpainted mammy and cook shakers. The roly-poly set is unmarked and shows considerable wear. The slender set is marked Japan. Circa 1st pr.-early 1940's, 2nd pr.-late 1940's. (all 4¼")

Attractive pair of shakers on matching tray. The shakers are decorated with a happy woman carrying a basket on one arm and a melon under the other arm. They have "Nassau" written on the back side. Marked-Royal Winton, made in England. Circa 1960's. (tray-6" long, shakers-2⅜")

First pair of shakers shown is a small, unusual cook and maid set of Japanese ceramic. The second set is an unmarked cook and mammy in a small size. Circa 1st pr.-1950's, 2nd pr.-1940's. (3¼", 3¼")

Easiest to find black salt and pepper sets are the mammy and cook pairs in the 4 inch to 5 inch range. Dozens of different color combinations are available to the collector. They were made both in Japan and the U.S.A. The black pair with white aprons and orange hats and spoons are the only pair marked-#ok Japan. Circa mid-1940's to 1950's.

Four piece ceramic spice set in original wooden rack. The containers are shaped like male cooks. Marked-made in Japan. Paper label-Fred Roberts Company, San Francisco. Circa 1950's. (3¼" tall, rack 10½" long)

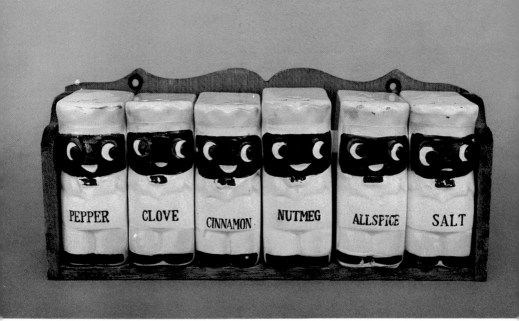

Black cook, six piece ceramic spice set in original wooden rack. Marked-Japan. Circa 1950's. (3¼" tall, rack 8¾" long)

Charming ceramic spice jars are decorated with molded cooks and mammys. Each jar has a different colored top. Marked Japan. Circa 1950's. (3")

Three piece ceramic spice set in the shape of women holding bouquets of flowers. No marks. Circa 1955-1960. (6")

Cute wooden pair of shakers called Rastus and Lisa. Circa 1940's. (2¾")

White ceramic shakers, decorated with a molded cook and mammy, fill from the bottom. No marks. Circa 1950's. (3")

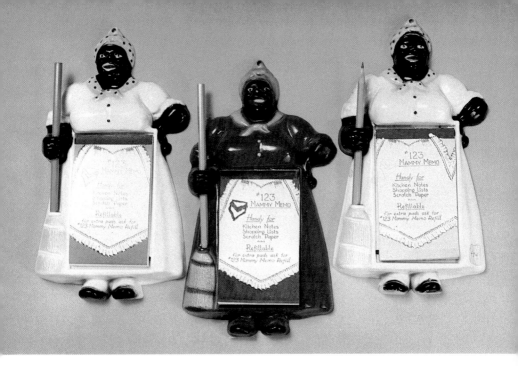

Mammy memo #123, made of lightweight plastic, came in many different color combinations to match any kitchen decor. It can be found marked either-made in U.S.A.-or-NORLEANS made in Greece. Circa mid-1940's-1950's. (10¼")

Pair of colorful painted chalkware memo pads in the shape of a mammy and cook. Circa 1940's. (9" to 9¾")

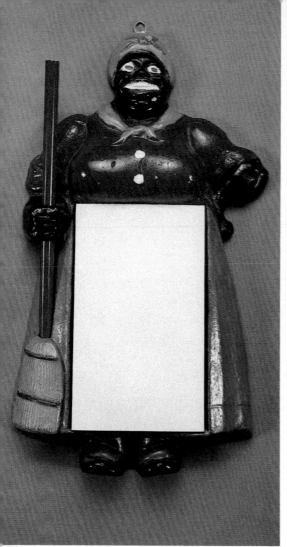

Early mammy kitchen memo pad made of resin-coated composition. It received a U.S. design patent filed by Samuel Brodsky of Brooklyn, N.Y. on Mary 28, 1940. A matching black chef memo pad was also patented by Mr. Brodsky in 1940. Marked Mammy Memo Reg. U.S. Pat. Off. Made in U.S.A. Hampden Novelty Mfg. Co. Inc., Holyoke, Mass. Pat. no. D120724. Circa early 1940's. (10¼")

Grinning black chef memo pad matches mammy memo #123. It is made of lightweight plastic and can be found in other colors, including blue and green. Marked-ABN 32 Norleans made in Greece. (10¼")

Another type of plastic mammy memo pad. Notice the difference between this pad and Mammy Memo #123. No marks. (9½")

Cute young mammy note pad and potholder combination is made of painted chalkware. (9")

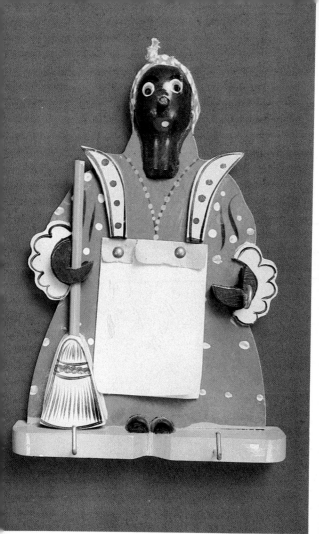

Painted wooden mammy memo pad, keyholder and potholder combination made a helpful kitchen accessory. It also came in blue. Circa 1940's. (10½")

Wooden note pad cut in the shape of a mammy. She is wearing a green polka dot kerchief. Her arms form the holder for the roll of notepaper. Marked with paper tag-Standard Specialty, Finest, made in Japan. Circa 1940's. (10½")

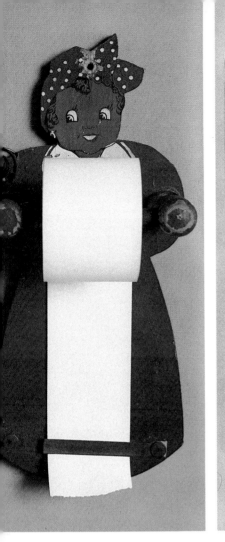

Wooden note pad cut in the shape of a mammy. She is wearing a red dress and red polka dot kerchief. No marks. Circa 1940's. (10″)

Mammy with a string tied around her finger is pictured on the wooden "I'se Gotta Git —" grocery reminder board with 24 items. Circa 1940's and 1950's. (11″)

A frowning mammy, a question mark, and a telephone are pictured on this wooden grocery reminder board with 24 items. (10″)

APPLES	MEAT
BREAD	MILK
BUTTER	ORANGES
CEREAL	ONIONS
COFFEE	POTATOES
CRACKERS	RICE
EGGS	SALT
EXTRACTS	SPICES
FLOUR	SOAP
LARD	SUGAR
LEMONS	TEA
MATCHES	TOMATOES

Smiling young boy and girl chalkware potholders are holding large slices of watermelon. (3¾″)

APPLES	LEMONS
BANANAS	MATCHES
BREAD	MEAT
BUTTER	MILK
CEREAL	ORANGES
COFFEE	RICE
CRACKERS	SALT
EGGS	SPICES
EXTRACTS	SOAP
FLOUR	SUGAR
LARD	TEA

Small, wooden grocery reminder board with only 22 items features a red-lipped mammy tapping her head with her finger. "Reckon Ah Needs?" (8")

Painted chalkware pair of hanging potholders in the shape of a mammy and cook. Circa late 1940's. (6")

• APPLES	• MATCHES
• BACON	• MEAT
• BREAD	• MILK
• BUTTER	• ONIONS
• CEREAL	• ORANGES
• COFFEE	• PEPPER
• CRACKERS	• POTATOES
• EGGS	• RICE
• FLOUR	• SALT
• LARD	• SUGAR
• LEMONS	• TEA
• LETTUCE	• TOMATOES

Mammy with her finger touching her head decorates the "We Needs?" varnished plywood grocery reminder board with 24 items. A similar kitchen reminder was sold in 1943 by Sears for 29 cents. (11")

Round wooden plaque with a cut out of a mammy decorating it, is a hanging pot holder. Marked-made in occupied Japan. Circa 1945-1952. (5")

Large wooden "I Hasta Have" grocery reminder board with 49 items features a mammy with crossed arms. Circa 1940's. (11½")

"I HASTA HAVE"

FLOUR	SHORTENING	MEAT
MEAL	CHEESE	FISH
RICE	BUTTER	BACON
CEREAL	EGGS	BREAD
MACARONI	MILK	CRACKERS
SUGAR	JUICES	CAKE
SALT	RAISINS	SOUPS
PEPPER	PRUNES	VINEGAR
SPICES	MAYONNAISE	LEMONS
SODA	RELISHES	STARCH
B. POWDER	PICKLES	CLEANSER
TEA	JELLY	SOAP
COFFEE	GELATINE	T. TISSUE
CHOCOLATE	SAUCES	P. TOWELS
EXTRACTS	KETCHUP	MATCHES

FRESH VEGETABLES
CANNED VEGETABLES
FRESH FRUIT
CANNED FRUIT

Wall hanging potholders in the shape of a boy and girl sharing a slice of watermelon. The painted chalkware is worn in many places. Circa 1940's. (4")

Decorative pair of painted chalkware potholders are in excellent condition. The little girl is carrying a green umbrella and the matching boy a yellow umbrella. (7¾")

Set of painted chalkware potholders in the shape of a grinning little boy and girl with large eyes and lips holding a piece of watermelon. Circa late 1940's. (5¼")

Humorous set of hanging chalkware plaques, frowning man and smiling mammy, were used as kitchen decoration. Circa 1940's. (3½" & 3")

Detailed pair of chalkware plaques in the shape of a woman wearing a red hat and a man wearing a yellow straw hat. Circa 1950's. (5¼")

Small, matched set of chalkware plaques in the shape of a man and woman. The woman has a gold metal earring in her ear. Circa 1950's. (3¼" & 2⅝")

Linen dish towel is decorated with a lithographed print of children eating watermelons. Circa 1940's. (15" x 28½")

Lithographed, linen dish towel pictures a black man on a porch playing a banjo with dancing children. The lithographed linen towels can be found in a variety of designs. Circa 1940's. (14½" x 30")

Linen tablecloth is decorated with a lithographed picture of a pair of happy mammies dancing. Circa late 1940's to early 1950's. (52")

Charming set of six hand-embroidered dish towels show a mammy doing various household chores with the questionable help of her small son. Circa 1940's.

Sugar bowl or grease pot in the brown glazed clown pattern shaped like a tea-kettle. Matching salt and pepper shakers are also available. Circa 1950's. (4½")

Dish towel with an embroidered and appliqued mammy ringing a dinnerbell was hand-done. Circa 1930's-1940's.

Cardboard mammy serving pancakes, wearing a red blouse and a cloth skirt is a toaster cover. Circa 1950's. (16")

Mammy toaster cover of cloth and styrene is wearing a cream dress printed with red tulips, matching turban, and white apron. Circa 1940's to 1950's.

Machine and hand-stitched appliqued and embroidered linen dish towel is decorated with a mammy carrying baskets. Circa 1940's. (22" long)

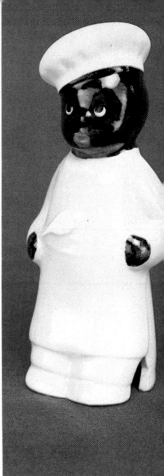

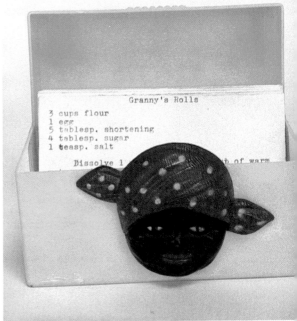

Granny's Rolls

3 cups flour
1 egg
5 tablesp. shortening
4 tablesp. sugar
1 teasp. salt

Dissolve 1 ___ of warm

These three mammy doll laundry bags are an example of the many color combinations that can be found. Circa 1940's to 1950's. (16½", 17", 16½")

Black cook wearing yellow and holding a spoon in one hand is a ceramic piebird. It also came in green. No marks. Circa 1950's. (4½")

Black cook with his hands in his trouser pockets is a Toby mug. Marked-Made in Japan. Circa 1945-1955. (3½")

Plastic recipe box has a molded mammy face on the front. It was made by Fosta and came in yellow, red, green, and blue. No marks. Circa early 1950's. (3½")

Plastic measuring spoon set and chalkware holder. The holder is shaped like a mammy, dressed in bright red, yellow, and green, holding a large basket. No marks. Circa 1940's. (5¾")

Wooden matchholder with the front piece cut out like a mammy. She is dressed in green and white. No marks. Circa 1930's-early 1940's. (7½")

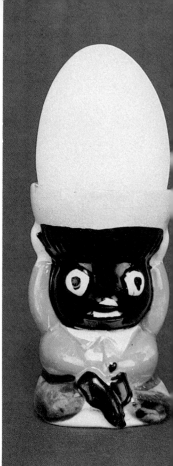

Mammy No. 20 self-starting electric clock by Lanshire. The mammy, wearing a blue striped apron holding the clock, was designed by Charles E. Murphy and made by Red Wing Potteries, Inc. of Red Wing Minnesota. Possibility of warehouse find. (10")

Little boy sitting with his hands over his head dressed in blue and orange is a ceramic egg cup. Hard to find. No marks. Circa 1940's. (2½")

Large ceramic spoon rest shaped like a mammy dressed in blue and white has places for two spoons. No marks. Circa late 1950's. (8")

Ceramic mammy spoon rests in two sizes are not marked. Circa 1950's. (8½" & 6")

Two cute black cook egg-timers in excellent condition. The white dressed cook is unmarked. The black cook is marked-Occupied Japan. Circa 1945-1952. (3½", 3¼")

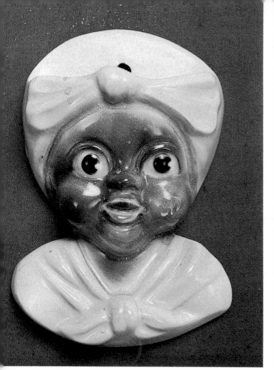

Brown-skinned mammy dressed all in yellow is a wall-hung scouring pad holder. It was made by Coventry Ware, Inc. of Barberton, Ohio. Marked 5601A, Coventry, made in the U.S.A. Circa late 1940's-1950's. (5")

Yellow, ceramic, stove-shaped planter has a mammy dressed in white perched on the top. It was available in several colors. A similar washing machine with mammy was also made. No marks. Circa 1940's. (5½")

Matching ceramic tea set including a mammy with black face and purple lips teapot, little boy sugar bowl and little girl creamer. The teapot and sugar bowl have lids. Marked-Japan. Circa 1945-1955. (3¼", 4¼", 3")

Yellow dressed mammy is a wall pocket. A matching black chef was also available. No marks. Circa 1950's. (5")

Wall planter made of ceramic is very detailed. Marked-Japan. Circa late 1940's-1950's. (5¾")

Souvenir teacup with a lady carrying a basket over one arm and a melon under the other. Marked-Royal Winton, made in England. Circa 1960's.

Hard to find black mammy creamer is dressed in a white apron and holding a red spoon. Marked-c# Cameo China Co. Wellsville, Ohio. Circa 1949-1952. (3¼")

Mammy teapot with a brown face and pastel pink lips. Marked-Occupied Japan. Circa 1945-1952. (4¼")

Adorable matching pair of ceramic planters. The little girl is holding an ear of corn against her pink dress. The little boy, dressed in overalls, is holding an ear of corn over his shoulder. Both marked-Japan. Circa late 1940's-1950's. (5", 5⅛")

Colorful, well-detailed planter is shaped like a young boy sitting with his back against a tree eating a slice of watermelon. Marked-Made in Japan. Circa 1950's. (5")

Man with boat ceramic planter was a piece in the McCoy Calypso
line. Marked McCoy. (10½" x 5½")

McCoy Calypso line ceramic planter. Man playing guitar is
leaning against a large barrel. Marked-McCoy. (7" x 5")

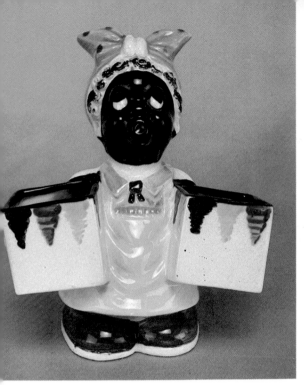

Young mammy looking up is a ceramic holder for matches or toothpicks. No marks. Circa 1940's-1950's. (5½")

Ceramic soap or scouring pad holder shaped like a mammy holding out her arms. No marks. Circa 1940's. (5⅛")

Yarn mammy doll dinner bell was sold in New Orleans as a souvenir. No marks.

Ceramic kitchen wall plaque or spoonrest that looks like a smiling mammy rolling her eyes. Marked-Japan. Circa 1950's. (7½")

Three small cast iron, skillet shaped kitchen ashtrays. Marked-John Wright Inc. Circa 1950's. (4½", 5¾", 4½")

Two small ceramic bells shaped like a cook and mammy. The cook trimmed in gold was made in Japan. The mammy bell is unmarked. (3½", 3") Sometimes mistaken for a toothpick holder, this young mammy dressed in white and yellow is a candlestick. Unmarked. Circa 1950's. (5½")
Brushes with painted wooden tops came in a wide range of sizes. Unmarked. Circa 1930's-1940's. (7" & 4½")

Ceramic mammy dressed in white with a red, white, and blue apron is a bell. Marked-Fred Hinode. Circa mid 1940's-1950's. (4")

Old metal bottle opener shaped like a grinning black man, wearing a bowtie. The opener has been reproduced. (4")

Mammy cloth doll sewing kit with felt back and apron. It has a hand embroidered face and apron. The doll had places for a thimble, scissors, and other sewing needs. Circa 1940's. (9")

Souvenir pin cushion features a small painted bisque boy eating watermelon seated atop a red polka dot cushion. Circa 1930's. (2⅝")

Large mammy pin cushion with painted pottery top and colorful cloth skirt and apron. Circa 1930's. (6")

Rare ceramic mammy wall lamp. The superbly detailed mammy is wearing a white turban and a red and white checked scarf. Original fixtures. No marks. Attributed U.S.A. (7")

Three charming clothe dolls with stitched faces. The two mammy dolls are wearing metal hoop earrings. The little girl doll has yarn hair braided. Circa 1930's-1950's. (14",17",18")

Little boy holding a bottle of milk and leaning against a watermelon is a cute pin cushion. Marked-Japan. Circa 1940's. (2½")

Painted metal travel sewing kit. The weighted bottom unscrews to reveal thread, needle, and thimble. (2")

Black cloth doll holding a pin cushion has an embroidered face. Circa 1930's. (4½")

Mammy pin cushion with wooden head and pipe cleaner arms is dressed in a red polkadot dress. Marked Japan. (5")

New Orleans souvenir clothe doll with felt features is wearing a red hat and overalls. (7")

Colorful, tin, battery-operated toy. The smiling man with hinged legs dances. Attributed Japan. Circa 1950's. (10½")

Topsy Turvey clothe doll with stitched faces. When one doll is up the other doll is hidden by the skirt. (12″)

Engaging pair of painted bisque dolls that have tufts of real hair mixed with molded hair. Marked-Japan. Circa late 1940's-1950's. (2½")

Two tiny cast iron dolls with handpainted features and clothing. Some paint wear. Circa 1920's. (7/8" & 6/8")

Original, old *Jolly Nigger* painted cast iron bank. To operate first a penny was placed in his hand, then the bank lever was turned. As the money was deposited in his mouth his eyes and ears moved. Reproductions of this bank marked Taiwan can be found. (6")

Tin wind-up toy called the *Charleston Trio* was patented on Oct. 1, 1921 by Louis Marx & Co. of New York. The large center figurine dances, the other plays the fiddle, and the dog carries a cane. (9")

94

Tin wind-up toy called *Sweeping Mammy* was made in the U.S.A. by Lindstrom of Bridgeport, Conn. (8")

Ceramic pincushion shaped like a little boy sitting. The top of the hat holds the pin cushion. Marked-made in Japan. Circa 1930's and 1940's. (2¾")

Lucky Joe Bank, shaped like Joe Lewis, was sold originally containing Nash's Prepared Mustard. The bank received a U.S. design patent on Dec. 27, 1938. (4¼")

Repainted, old mammy shaped cast iron bank. Reproductions available. (6")

Beautiful, double-sided, old, cast iron bank shaped like a young girl wearing a hat. (4½")

Old, painted, metal, mammy doorstop and bank. Reproductions available. (9" & 5½")

 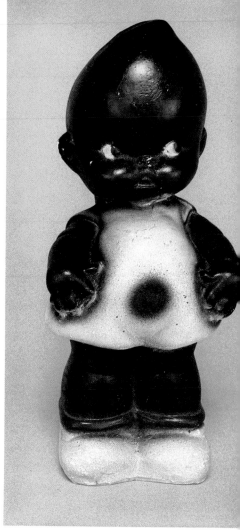

Old, chalkware, carnival give-a-way shaped like a seated, bare-foot black boy has excellent detail. Minor chipping. (12¼")

Cute, chalkware, carnival give-a-way bank is shaped like a girl kewpie doll. On her back is a pair of wings. (12")

Ceramic mammy bank, with the coin slot in the back, in two handpainted versions. No marks. Late 1940's (6½")

Five piece, ceramic band includes a violinist, accordion player, drummer, bass player, and banjo player. All five pieces are marked-occupied Japan. Circa 1945-1952. (smallest 4¼"-tallest 5")

Small ceramic, five piece band includes a fiddle player, harmonica player, drummer, banjo player, and a trumpet player. Marked Handpainted Japan. Circa 1950's. (smallest 2¾"-tallest 3¼")

Front and back pictures of a doublesided ceramic figurine. The comical figure is a man before marriage and after. There is also a before and after marriage woman figurine. Paper label-Japan. Circa 1950's. (5")

Two different finished versions of the same shoe shine boy. Both marked-Japan. Circa 1940's. (4¼")

Amos & Andy, chalkware, carnival give-away figurine. Some chipping and flaking of paint. (12")

Little boy statuette needs his fishing pole to finish the picture. No marks. Circa 1950's. (8")

Painted ceramic figurine of a little black boy sitting on a chamberpot. No marks. (4")

Common bisque outhouse showing one boy on the commode and the other boy looking inside. There are many different figurines with this theme. Made in Japan. Circa 1940's. (2¼")

Young black boys replace the usual monkeys acting out the famous saying "Speak no evil, see no evil." This bisque figurine is hard to find. The painted finish is very worn.

Attractive pair of ceramic choirboys dressed in white robes trimmed in gold. One is holding a candle, the other a book. There are two other matching choirboys available. One is holding a star, the other has his hands in prayer, Marked-Japan. Circa 1945-1955. (5¼")

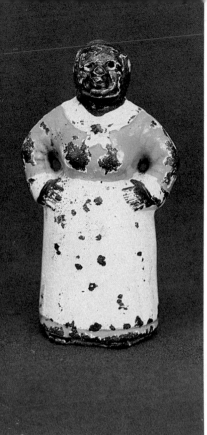

Mammy dressed in blue and white is a cast iron paperweight. The original paint shows wear. No marks. (2½")

Weathered concrete yard ornament shaped like a seated boy eating watermelon. (12¾")

Cast iron mammy is wearing a
red dress and a bright yellow
shawl. A hole in the top of her
hand indicates she was probably
attached to something else at one
time. (4½")

Cigarette box of cedar wood is
decorated with a bell boy in red
uniform. Marked-J.B. Deere Cedar-
craft 1052 62. Circa 1930's. (7¼"
x 5")

Black train porter carrying a bag is a metal miniature. (1")

Colorful clown decanter with matching shot glasses is made of red clay. Marked-Pat. Pend. Paper label-Thames, hand painted. Japan. 1950's (8½", 2")

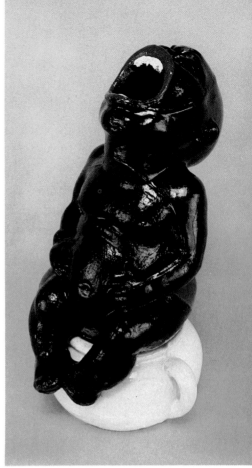

Heavy metal paperweight is shaped like a black caddy carrying a full bag of clubs. No marks. (6½")

Young black boy seated on a chamberpot, holding his stomach screaming in pain is a metal incense burner. restored paint. Marked-National Products Inc., Chicago,Ill. Circa 1920's-1930's. (6")

Heart-shaped covered box. The lid is decorated with a three dimensional man's face, which is highly detailed, and four roses. The bottom is trimmed in matching roses. Marked-made in Japan. (4")

Two composition thermometers, one shaped like a little boy with his pants pulled down and the other a little girl also with her pants lowered. The boy is fairly common, the little girl is hard to find. Boy circa 1949. Girl circa 1955. Both marked Multi Products Inc. (5½" & 5")

Ceramic Butler wine decanter. The ceramic head has a cork stopper. Wine was served through the corked bottle held out in the butler's hand. No marks. Hard to find. (7⅛") Circa late 1930's to 1941.

Hard working mammy has her breast caught in the wringer of this washing machine ashtray. Marked c# 1953 Plastic Arts. (5")

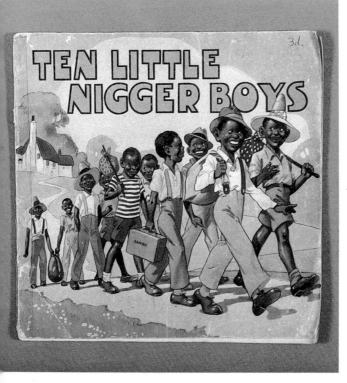

TEN LITTLE
NIGGER BOYS

3d.

ASHES.

Two hand-painted ceramic liquor bottles with ceramic and cork stoppers. The first bottle is decorated with an embossed man holding a bottle. The paper label on the side reads, "Jungle juice, Distilled sin, this juice is sex years old, bottled in barn." The second bottle is embossed with a bar and bartender. Both marked Hand Painted Japan. 1950's (8½")

Ceramic ashtray shaped like a boy's face with his mouth wide open and his tongue hanging out. Marked-Japan. Circa 1950's. (4")

Many different editions of *Ten Little Nigger Boys* can be found. This one was published in England and received copyright No.9910. (9½")

Little boy hauling a wagon is a small ceramic ashtray. Easy to find. Several versions available. Marked-Japan. Circa mid 1940's-1950's. (1½")

Metal pin advertising the Montrose Watermelon Festival of 1951 is decorated with a little boy eating watermelon. (2¼")

Souvenir, wooden naughty is shaped like an outhouse, when you open the door marked "Private", the revealed mammy tells you to "Quit yo Peeking". Circa 1950's. (4¾")

113

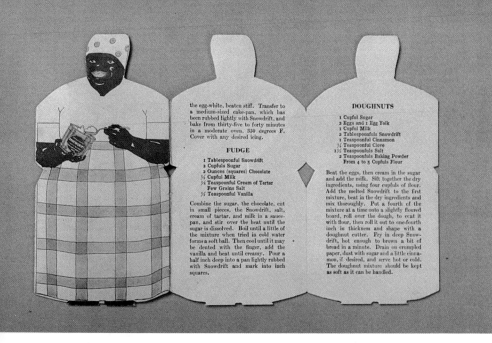

Paper mammy shaped fold-out recipe book given to customers who bought Snowdrift shortening.

Metal nodder ashtray. The ashtray is decorated with nodding figurine shaped like a little black boy holding his tummy after trying a cigar. No marks. (4")

Two ceramic ashtrays shaped like bedpans with little naked black boys sitting on them. The first is marked-Japan, the other is unmarked. Circa 1940's. (3")

Little Black Sambo two record set with book was narrated by Don Lyon and distributed by Columbia Records. Circa 1950's. (10")

The recipe book *Southern Cook Book* was copyrighted by Lillie Lustig, Claire Sondheim, and Sarah Rensel in 1939. (9¼")

The recipe book *Southern Cook Book of Fine Old Dixie Recipes* was copyrighted by Lillie Lustig, Claire Sondhelm, and Sarah Rensel in 1935. The book was published by Culinary Arts Press of Reading, Pa. (9¼")

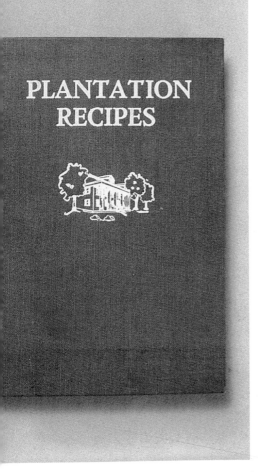

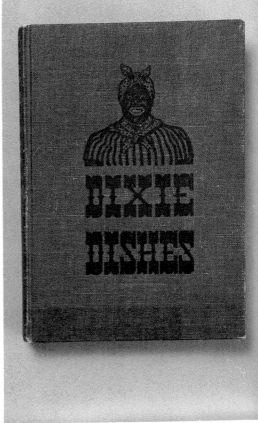

The book *Plantation Recipes* written by Lessie Bowers and published by Robert Speller & Sons of New York was copyrighted in 1959. The author's grandmother was a slave on a South Carolina plantation and taught her to cook. (8½")

Dixie Dishes, a book of traditional southern recipes, was copyrighted by Marion W. Flexner in 1941. It was published by the firm Hale, Cushman, & Flint of Boston. (7¾")

Animated book *Little Black Sambo* by Helen Bannerman was copyrighted in 1943. The animation was by Julian Wehr and it was published by Duenewald Printing Inc., New York.

The 1938 edition of *Epaminondas and His Auntie* was written by Sara Cone Bryant and published by Riverside Press of Cambridge, Mass. It was illustrated by Inez Hogan.

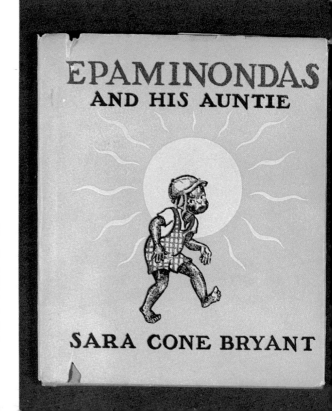

The book *Senegambian Sizzles* written by E.V. White and illustrated by Leta Nae Calhoun was published in 1945 by Banks Upshaw & Co., Dallas. The original price was $2.00.

The M.A. Donohue & Co. of Chicago 1919 edition of *Little Black Sambo* originally sold for 75 cents. (7½")

The children's book *Ten Little Nigger Boys* was published in Great Britain by Valentine and Sons Ltd. and received British Patent-No. 23379/1913. (9½")

Turky Trott by Kate Dyer and illustrated by Janet Robson was published by Platt & Munk Co. Inc. in 1942.

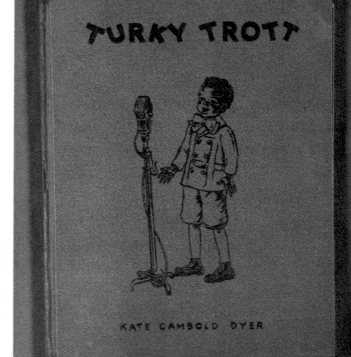

Menu cut in the shape of a mammy serving a hot dinner was for the Old Dixie Restaurant in Los Angeles, Ca. (9½")

A book of humorous tales called *Coon Yarns* was copyrighted in 1909 by James Sullivan and published by M.J. Ivers Co. (7")

121

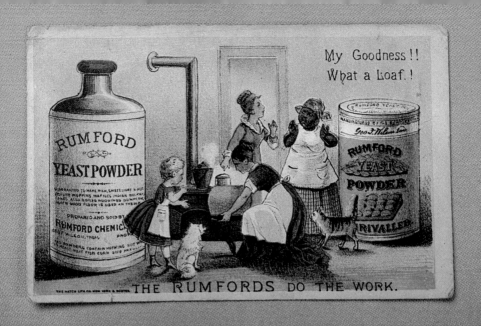

Humorous Trade Card for Rumford Yeast Powder. (5¼″ x 3¼″)

Blotter with advertising for *Mammy's delicious drumstix* pictures a mammy carrying a platter of chicken. (7¼″ x 3¼″)

Sheet music for the song *Carolina Mammy* by Billy James copyrighted in 1923. The cover claims the song was 'Successfully sung by Aunt Jemina. (9" x 12")

Humorous postcard of a black lady shopping for gloves by Tichnor Quality Views of Boston, Mass., Circa 1944-1952. 5½" x 3½")

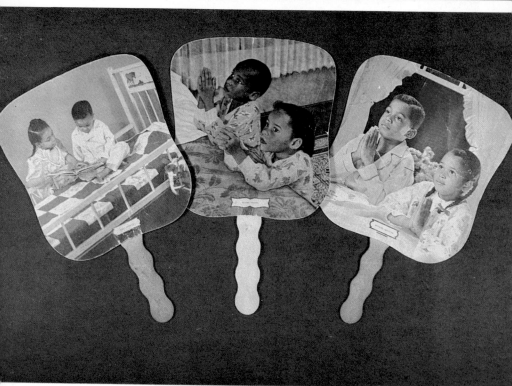

Six paper advertising fans with religious themes. The Fans have various companies advertising on the back and were usually given away free. Circa 1950's-1960's. (11½")

Cardboard advertising sign for Admiration Coffee shows mammy carrying a coffee service. Circa 1940's-1950's. (10¼")

Old Maid card game with 'Steppin' Sam' and 'Sassiety Sal' cards. (3½" x 2¼")

Funny, colorful valentines were printed in Germany. Circa 1930's-1950's. (7", 6½")

Down South decal featuring a smiling mammy was for hard finish type luggage or opaque surfaces. It was manufactured by Lindgren-Turner Co. of Spokane, Wash.

Amos and Andy
cardboard dolls
were copyrighted
in 1930 by the
Pepsodent Co.
Marked-Litho in
U.S.A. (8¼" &
7½")

Carolyn Chester's
round-base paper
doll called *Mammy
Cook and Her
Thanksgiving Dinner*
appeared in the
Nov. 1912 issue
of the Delineator.

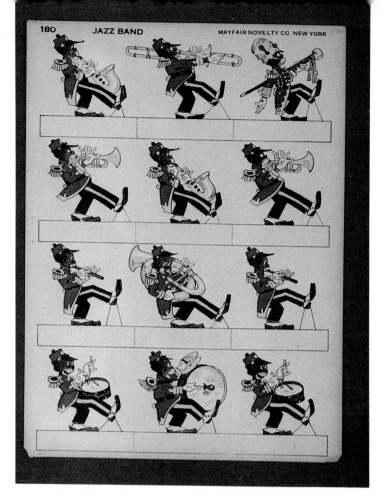

Twelve piece cardboard jazz band distributed by the Mayfair Novelty Co. of New York. Circa 1930's. (8" x 10½")

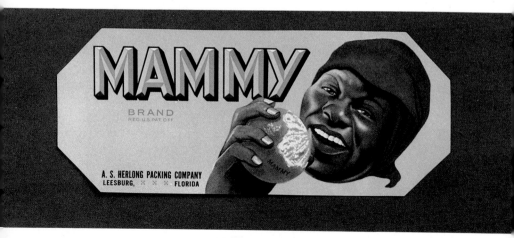

Advertising label for Mammy brand fruit used by the A.S. Herlong Packing Co. of Leesburg, Florida. (8½ x 3¾")

PATENTS

I hope the following United States Design Patents will be helpful to you the collector in dating items in your personal collection. All the Design Patents pictured are from the 1920's-1950's. In almost all cases, if an item received a design patent, it was manufactured.

70,525. TOY. Samuel Berger, New York, N. Y. Filed Sept. 26, 1921. Serial No. 503,405. Term of patent 7 years.

62,287. SMOKER STAND. Frederick E. Hadermann, New York, N. Y. Filed Oct. 15, 1921. Serial No. 508,022. Term of patent 3½ years.

The ornamental design for a toy substantially as shown.

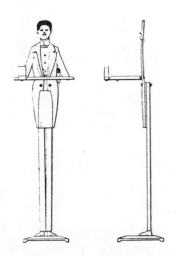

The ornamental design for smoker stand as shown and described.

63,467. DOLL. Valley M. Kieffer, Buffalo, N. Y. Filed Dec. 22, 1921. Serial No. 524,314. Term of patent 3½ years.

The ornamental design for a doll, as shown.

61,880. TOY. FERDINAND STRAUSS, New York, N. Y. Filed July 25, 1922. Serial No. 3,196. Term of patent 7 years.

The ornamental design for a statuette as shown.

64,009. STATUETTE. JAMES B. HARRINGTON, Norfolk, Va. Filed Mar. 20, 1923. Serial No. 5,547. Term of patent 3½ years.

The ornamental design for a toy, as shown.

65,657. DOLL. THEODORE F. KOTTER, Hollis, N. Y. Filed Mar. 30, 1923. Serial No. 5,646. Term of patent 3½ years.

The ornamental design for a broom, as shown.

65,191. BROOM. MINNIE JENNINGS, Spartanburg, S. C. Filed May 10, 1924. Serial No. 9,548. Term of patent 3½ years.

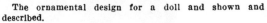

The ornamental design for a doll and shown and described.

69,559. TOY. SAMUEL BERGER, Newark, N. J. Filed May 17, 1924. Serial No. 9,635. Term of patent 14 years.

The ornamental design for a toy as shown.

66,841. DOLL. Katherine T. Donovan, Lynn, Mass. Filed May 26, 1924. Serial No. 9,708. Term of patent 3½ years.

The ornamental design for a doll as shown.

65,816. DOLL. Hubert E. Leland, New York, N. Y. Filed Aug. 11, 1924. Serial No. 10,439. Term of patent 3½ years.

68,115. DOLL. Mary Phipps, Mitchellville, Md. Filed May 19, 1925. Serial No. 13,489. Term of patent 3½ years.

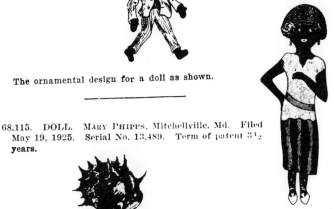

The ornamental design for a doll, as shown.

68,367. DOLL. Elizabeth G. Adrian, New York, N. Y. Filed July 13, 1925. Serial No. 14,075. Term of patent 7 years.

The ornamental design for a doll as shown.

The ornamental design for a doll, as shown.

72,470. GOAT AND DARKIE TOY. William D. Bludworth, Sacramento, Calif. Filed Jan. 2, 1926. Serial No. 15,987. Term of patent 3½ years.

The ornamental design for a goat and darkie toy, as shown.

69,900. FIGURE TOY. LOUIS MARX, Brooklyn, N. Y.
Filed Feb. 20, 1926. Serial No. 16,618. Term of
patent 3½ years.

The ornamental design for a figure toy, as shown.

73,281. SMOKER'S STAND. JOHN C. CRAMER, Dayton,
Ohio. Filed Apr. 13, 1927. Serial No. 21,578. Term
of patent 3½ years.

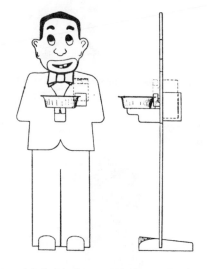

DOLL. CURTIS E. BATCHELOR, Oklahoma City,
Filed June 10, 1927. Serial No. 22,386. Term
of 7 years.

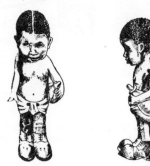

The ornamental design for a smoker's stand substantially as shown.

---

ornamental design for a doll as shown.

The ornamental design for a textile fabric or article
of similar nature, as shown.

**79,990. TEXTILE FABRIC OR ARTICLE OF SIMILAR
NATURE.** GRACE SELMA SAUER, New York, N. Y. Filed
Oct. 31, 1927. Serial No. 23,957. Term of patent
3½ years.

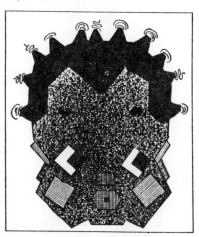

78,957. DOLL. MIRIAM N. NEUGASS, New York, N. Y.
Filed Feb. 19, 1929. Serial No. 30,128. Term of patent
14 years.

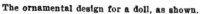

The ornamental design for a doll, as shown.

83,731. DOLL. KRESTINE KNUDSEN, Oakland, Calif. Filed Jan. 25, 1930. Serial No. 34,288. Term of patent 3½ years.

82,440. VEHICLE TOY. LOUIS MARX, New York, N. Y., assignor to Charles J. Correll and Freeman F. Gosden, Chicago, Ill. Filed Mar. 31, 1930. Serial No. 35,075. Term of patent 3½ years.

The ornamental design for a doll, substantially as shown.

The ornamental design for a vehicle toy, substantially as shown and described.

82,521. ASH RECEIVER. JOHN B. SCELZI, Hopewell, Va. Filed Apr. 3, 1930. Serial No. 35,144. Term of patent 7 years.

81,601. SMOKER'S STAND. JAMES A. SUTSH, Flint, Mich. Filed Apr. 17, 1930. Serial No. 35,295. Term of patent 7 years.

The ornamental design for an ash receiver as shown.

The ornamental design for a smoker's stand, as shown.

81,821. BOOK END. James A. Anderson, Minneapolis,
Minn. Filed May 24, 1930. Serial No. 35,762. Term
of patent 3½ years.

The ornamental design for a book end, as shown.

81,822. BOOK END. James A. Anderson, Minneapolis,
Minn. Filed May 24, 1930. Serial No. 35,763. Term
of patent 3½ years.

The ornamental design for a book end, as shown.

82,980. SMOKER'S STAND OR SIMILAR ARTICLE.
Lilly Daigre-Gore, New Orleans, La. Filed July 7,
1930. Serial No. 36,292. Term of patent 14 years.

The ornamental design for a smoker's stand or similar
article, as shown and described.

85,464. WALKING TOY. FRANCIS J. CATTERLIN, Los Angeles, Calif. Filed July 21, 1930. Serial No. 36,422. Term of patent 3½ years.

87,969. FIGURE TOY. LOUIS MARX, New York, N. Y., assignor to Charles J. Correll and Freeman F. Gosden. Chicago, Ill. Filed Mar. 12, 1931. Serial No. 39,040. Term of patent 14 years.

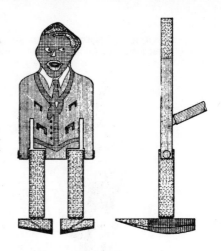

The ornamental design for a walking toy, substantially as shown and described.

87,970. FIGURE TOY. LOUIS MARX, New York, N. Y., assignor to Charles J. Correll and Freeman F. Gosden, Chicago, Ill. Filed Mar. 12, 1931. Serial No. 39,041. Term of patent 14 years.

The ornamental design for a figure toy, substantially as shown.

84,757. SMOKER'S STAND. CLARA SAFFOLD, Los Angeles, Calif. Filed May 1, 1931. Serial No. 39,678. Term of patent 7 years.

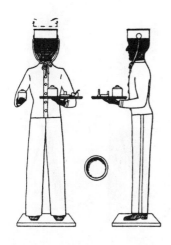

The ornamental design for a figure toy, substantially as shown.

The ornamental design for a smoker's stand substantially as shown.

87,648. LAWN SPRINKLER. Roy H. Sherbondy and Ray E. Sherbondy, Akron, Ohio. Filed Aug. 19, 1931. Serial No. 40,892. Term of patent 14 years.

The ornamental design for a lawn sprinkler as shown.

86,760. COMBINED TABLE AND RACK. Rudolph Berliner, Los Angeles, Calif. Filed Oct. 28, 1931. Serial No. 41,552. Term of patent 3½ years.

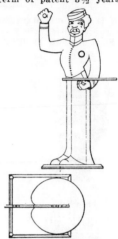

The ornamental design for a combined table and rack as shown.

86,603. STATUETTE OR SIMILAR ARTICLE. Frederick H. House, Buffalo, N. Y., assignor to Jacob House & Sons, Buffalo, N. Y., a Partnership. Filed Jan. 14, 1932. Serial No. 42,475. Term of patent 7 years.

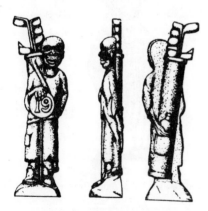

The ornamental design for a statuette or similar article, substantially as shown.

87,413. COMBINED DOLL OR SIMILAR ARTICLE AND SUPPORT FOR SAME. Henry M. Rundle, Glen Ridge, N. J. Filed Apr. 30, 1932. Serial No. 43,666. Term of patent 14 years.

The ornamental design for a combined doll or similar article and support for same, substantially as shown.

89,004. FIGURE TOY. HARRY JOHN WILLIAMS, Zephyr-hills, Fla. Filed Oct. 19, 1932. Serial No. 45,418. Term of patent 3½ years.

89,823. HOLDER FOR A THERMOMETER OR THE LIKE. JESSIE H. MC'CREARY, Anderson, Ind. Filed Feb. 23, 1933. Serial No. 47,302. Term of patent 7 years.

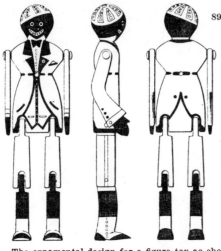

The ornamental design for a figure toy as shown.

The ornamental design for a holder for a thermometer, or the like, as shown and described.

93,796
DESIGN FOR A KITCHEN NOVELTY MAID
Florence E. Rocus, Santa Barbara, Calif.
Application May 5, 1933, Serial No. 48,020
Term of patent 7 years

The ornamental design for a kitchen novelty maid, as shown.

97,092
DESIGN FOR A RAG DOLL
Léda Hincks Plauché, New Orleans, La.
Application May 28, 1935, Serial No. 57,058
Term of patent 3½ years

The ornamental design for a rag doll, as shown.

100,187
DESIGN FOR A FIGURE TOY
Lawrence R. Adrian, Iowa City, Iowa
Application April 15, 1936, Serial No. 62,139
Term of patent 3½ years

100,752
DESIGN FOR A SMOKER'S STAND
Louis V. Aronson, Newark, N. J., assignor to Art
Metal Works, Inc., a corporation of New
Jersey
Application June 13, 1936, Serial No. 63,273
Term of patent 3½ years

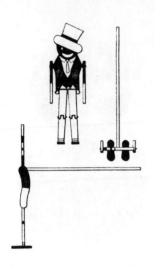

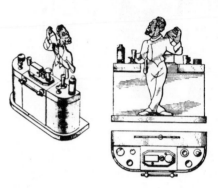

The ornamental design for a figure toy as
shown.

The ornamental design for a smoker's stand
substantially as shown.

102,428
**DESIGN FOR A COMBINED ASHTRAY AND
CIGARETTE CONTAINER**
Maxon Lester Graham, Seattle, Wash.
Application November 3, 1936, Serial No. 65,684
Term of patent 3½ years

103,518
DESIGN FOR A DANCING TOY FIGURE
Kelly C. Sears, Rural Hall, N. C.
Application December 15, 1936, Serial No. 66,54
Term of patent 7 years

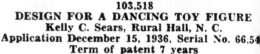

The ornamental design for a combined ashtray
and cigarette container, as shown.

The ornamental design for a dancing toy fig
ure, as shown.

109,978
DESIGN FOR A DANCING DOLL
Clarence Leon Craven, Detroit, and Silvester Ciccone and Jay G. Miller, Highland Park, Mich.
Application March 3, 1938, Serial No. 75,562
Term of patent 7 years

110,119
DESIGN FOR A GIFT NOVELTY
Mae A. Glazebrook, Memphis, Tenn.
Application October 16, 1937, Serial No. 72,245
Term of patent 3½ years

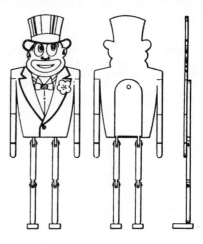

The ornamental design for a dancing doll, as shown.

The ornamental design for a gift novelty, as shown.

114,404
DESIGN FOR A COMBINED DOLL AND VANITY, BAG OR SIMILAR ARTICLE
Gretchen v. B. Menken, New York, N. Y.
Application July 22, 1938, Serial No. 78,644
Term of patent 7 years

The ornamental design for a combined doll and vanity bag or similar article, substantially as shown.

113,226
DESIGN FOR A GIFT NOVELTY
Joseph Hollander, Baton Rouge, La.
Application October 18, 1938, Serial No. 80,522
Term of patent 14 years

The ornamental design for a gift novelty, as shown.

The ornamental design for a combined Dinah and darning kit, substantially as shown.

113,234
DESIGN FOR A COMBINED DINAH DOLL AND DARNING KIT
James F. McDonald, Tulsa, Okla.
Application November 12, 1938, Serial No. 81,042
Term of patent 7 years

123,479
DESIGN FOR A CASE FOR CLOCKS OR SIMILAR ARTICLES
Frederick E. Greene, Westport, Conn., assignor to The Sessions Clock Company, Forestville, Conn., a corporation of Connecticut
Application May 9, 1940, Serial No. 92,241
Term of patent 14 years

124,723
DESIGN FOR A SIGN
Isaac J. Leavitt, Denver, Colo.
Application May 24, 1940, Serial No. 92,573
Term of patent 7 years

The ornamental design for a case for clocks or similar articles, substantially as shown.

The ornamental design for a sign, as shown.

129,606
DESIGN FOR A DANCING FIGURE TOY
Roy L. Paxton, Decatur, Ill.
Application April 15, 1941, Serial No. 100,395
Term of patent 3½ years

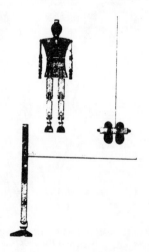

127,908
DESIGN FOR A SOUVENIR TEA BELL
Joseph Hollander, Baton Rouge, La.
Application April 21, 1941, Serial No. 100,543
Term of patent 14 years

The ornamental design for a dancing figure toy, as shown.

The ornamental design for a souvenir tea bell, as shown.

139,084
DESIGN FOR A FIGURINE
Catherine Miller McCullough, Miami, Fla.
Application July 19, 1944, Serial No. 114,455
Term of patent 3½ years
(Cl. D29—23)

The ornamental design for a figurine, substantially as shown.

139,085
DESIGN FOR A FIGURINE
Catherine Miller McCullough, Miami, Fla.
Application July 19, 1944, Serial No. 114,456
Term of patent 3½ years
(Cl. D29—23)

The ornamental design for a figurine, substantially as shown.

140,378
**DESIGN FOR A COMBINATION DOLL, DRESS-
ING TABLE, AND LAUNDRY BAG**
Natalie Kropatkin, Bronx County, N. Y.
Application November 9, 1944, Serial No. 116,251
Term of patent 7 years
(Cl. 33—6)

The ornamental design for a combination doll, dressing table, and laundry bag, substantially as shown.

144,044
DESIGN FOR A DANCING TOY
James H. Fannin, Everett, Wash.
Application March 13, 1945, Serial No. 118,449
Term of patent 3½ years
(Cl. D34—15)

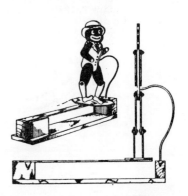

The ornamental design for a dancing toy, as shown.

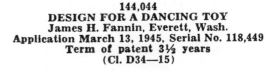

144,697
DESIGN FOR AN ALARM DEVICE OR
SIMILAR ARTICLE
Clarence E. Custard, Fulton, Mo.
Application June 14, 1945, Serial No. 120,105
Term of patent 7 years
(Cl. D72—1)

152,521
DESIGN FOR A TRAY
Naomi Mae Dean, Auxvasse, Mo.
Application May 28, 1947, Serial No. 139,331
Term of patent 14 years
(Cl. D44—10)

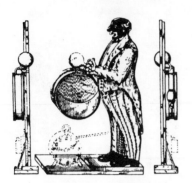

The ornamental design for an alarm device
or similar article, as shown and described.

The ornamental design for a tray, as shown.

146,166
DESIGN FOR AN ASH TRAY OR SIMILAR
ARTICLE
Pierre E. Bagur, Sr., New Orleans, La.
Application February 6, 1946, Serial No. 126,303
Term of patent 14 years
(Cl. D85—2)

155,574
DESIGN FOR A COMBINED RACK AND POT
HOLDERS OR SIMILAR ARTICLE
Samuel Brodsky, Brooklyn, N. Y.
Application October 29, 1947, Serial No. 142,187
Term of patent 14 years
(Cl. D44—24)

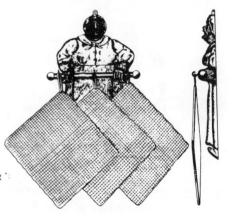

The ornamental design for an ash tray or similar article, as shown.

160,654
ASH TRAY
Marco Pagano, Buffalo, N. Y., assignor to
Ira L. Powsner, Buffalo, N. Y.
Application September 9, 1949, Serial No. 4,922
Term of patent 3½ years
(Cl. D85—2)

The ornamental design for a combined rack and pot holders or similar article, substantially as shown and described.

The ornamental design for an ash tray, substantially as shown.

163,974
COMBINED NOVELTY MIRROR AND WHISK BROOM
Ernest Steiner, New York, N. Y.
Application January 17, 1951, Serial No. 13,835
Term of patent 7 years
(Cl. D9—2)

163,975
NOVELTY FIGURE WHISK BROOM OR SIMILAR ARTICLE
Ernest Steiner, New York, N. Y.
Application January 17, 1951, Serial No. 13,836
Term of patent 7 years
(Cl. D9—2)

The ornamental design for a combined novelty mirror and whisk broom, substantially as shown and described.

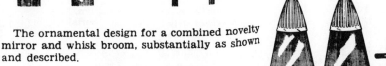

The ornamental design for a novelty figure whisk broom or similar article, substantially as shown.

170,287
BOTTLE
John B. Rosefield, Piedmont, Calif.
Application June 11, 1953, Serial No. 25,455
Term of patent 14 years
(Cl. D58—11)

The ornamental design for a bottle, as shown.

Picture Index

Price Guide

This price guide should be used as a very general guide to prices only. Local supply and demand of black collectibles will determine the prices in your area of the country. If the demand in your local region is high for black items expect to pay premium prices.

The prices stated are for items in mint condition. Deduct ten percent (10%) from the price for each ten percent of paint lost on plastic or ceramic items. Linens should be in good condition without holes, tears, stains, or faded areas.

Page	Position	Price	Page	Position	Price
1		$65-85		bottom left:	$25-45
2		$25		bottom right:	$10-20
3		$9-15	16	top:	$35
4	cookie:	$100-130		bottom: A.J.	$50
	mammy:	$150-200		U.M.	$45
5	large pr.:	$95-125		D. or W.	$25 each
	small pr.:	$45-65	17	top:	$7-12
6		$8-15		bottom: A.J.	$60
7		$45-65		U.M.	$50
8	top:	$20-25		D. or W.	$35 each
	bottom:	$35	18	left:	$200-300
9	left:	$15		right:	$25-45
	right:	$15	19	top: black face	$175-215
10	rack only:	$50-80		brown face	$190-230
11	cinnamon, paprika,			bottom:	$75-125
	nutmeg:	$30-38 each	20	top:	$100-125
	allspice, cloves,			bottom:	$110-150
	ginger:	$35-42 each	21	top:	$10-15
	rack only:	$150-225		bottom:	$125-150
12		$35-55	22	stove:	$750-1000
13	top:	$65-85		shaker:	$50
	bottom-with F & F		23	top:	$40-60
	symbol:	$35		bottom left:	$20-30
	bottom-without			bottom right:	$10-20
	symbol:	$25	24	top:	$15-20
14		$15-20		bottom left:	$80-95
15	top left-large pr.:	$45-55		bottom right:	$85-125
	top left-small pr.:	$30	25	top:	$20-25
	top right:	$12-18		bottom:	$125-150 pr.

Page	Position	Price	Page	Position	Price
26	top:	$15	49	top:	$20
	bottom:	$150-200		bottom left:	$18
27	top:	$8-12		bottom right:	$25
	bottom:	$65-75 pr.	50	top left:	15 pr.
28	top:	$60-90		top middle:	$25 pr.
	bottom:	$45-55		bottom left:	$45 pr.
29	top:	$50-75		bottom middle:	$55 pr.
	bottom:	$100-125	51	top:	$50-65 set
30	top:	$225-300		bottom left:	$25-30
	bottom:	$75 set		bottom right:	$20
31	top:	$175-250	52		$35 pr.
	bottom:	$55-65 set	53		$35 pr.
32	left:	$150-200	54	top:	$35-45 set
	right:	$75-110		bottom:	$35-45 set
33	top left:	$150-200	55	top:	$35-45 set
	top right:	$65-90		bottom:	$35-45 set
	bottom:	$85 set	56	top:	$18-20
34	top:	$300-400		bottom:	$20-30
	bottom:	$45-55 set	57	top: red	$50-60
35	top:	$85-125		top: other colors	$40-50
	bottom:	$45-60		bottom left:	$28
36	top left:	$125-200		bottom right:	$22
	top middle:	$150-200	58	left:	$25-30
	bottom: $12-15 pr.			right:	$20-30
37	top right:	$150-200	59	left:	$40-55
	bottom:	$25-45		right:	$35
38	left: new		60	left:	$20-25
	right:	$65-85		right:	$35
39	top:	$75-90	61	left:	$35
	bottom:	$30-45 pr.		right:	$45
40		$50-65	62	top:	$38
41	top left:	$55-75		bottom:	$20 pr.
	top right:	$45-55	63	top:	$45
	bottom left:	$45 pr.		bottom:	$22 pr.
	bottom right:	$30 pr.	64	top:	$35
42	top:	$55-75		bottom:	$20-25
	bottom: O. & U.		65	top:	$50
	set:	$85-100		bottom:	$12-20
	bottom: S. & P. set:	$35-40	66	top:	$18 each
43	top:	$30-35		bottom:	$12 each
	bottom:	$55-65	67	top:	$26 pr.
44	top left:	$45		bottom:	$28 pr.
	top right:	$45-65	68	top:	$28 pr
	bottom:	$35-40 set		bottom:	$30
45	top:	$95-110 pr.	69	top:	$30
	bottom: large pr.,	$85-95		bottom:	$75
	bottom: small pr.,	$30-35	70		$20 each
46	top:	$65-75	71	top:	$20 each
	bottom:	$35		bottom:	$15
47	top:	$45-65	72	top:	$35
	bottom:	$65-75		bottom:	$38-45
48	top left:	$35	73	top:	$25-30
	top right:	$40		bottom:	$35
	bottom left:	$18	74	top left:	$20-25
	bottom right:	$38		top right:	$35-45

Page	Position	Price	Page	Position	Price
	bottom left:	$20-25			box
	bottom right:	$125-150		bottom:	$20
75	left:	$55	96	top:	$12-15
	right:	$35-40		bottom:	$100
76	left:	$95-125	97	top:	$150-175
	right:	$25-30		bottom left:	$175-225
77	top left:	$28		bottom right:	$70
	top right: large	$38-45	98	left:	$90
	top right: small	$28-35		right:	$75
	bottom:	$25 each	99	left:	$20
78	top left:	$38-45		right:	$20
	top right:	$20-30	100	top:	$95 set
	bottom:	$125 set		bottom:	$60 set
79	top left:	$38-45	101		$40
	top right:	$45	102	left:	$25 each
	bottom:	$25		right:	$80
80	top:	$45	103	left:	$100
	bottom:	$90		right:	$40
81	top:	$38 each	104	top:	$10-20
	bottom:	$38-45		bottom:	$35-45
82	top:	$38-50	105		$20-25 each
	bottom:	$38-50	106	top:	$70
83	top left:	$38-45		bottom:	$100
	top right:	$35	107	top:	$70
	bottom:	$15		bottom:	$25
84	top:	$55-65	108	left:	$35
	bottom: small	$15		right:	$30-40
	large	$25	109	left:	$85
85	top left:	$20-28 each		right:	$60
	top right:	$35	110	top:	$85
	bottom: small	$15		bottom left:	$20
	large	$20		bottom right:	$25
86	left:	$35	111	left:	$125-150
	right:	$25		right:	$20
87	top left:	$15-20	112	top left:	$60 each
	top right:	$15-20		top right:	$15
	bottom left:	$20		bottom left:	$30
	bottom right:	$135-200		bottom right:	$10
88	left:	$45	113	left:	$15
	right:	$50		right:	$15
89	top:	$50	114	top:	$20
	bottom left:	$18		bottom:	$65
	bottom right:	$20	115	top:	$15-20 each
90	left:	$15		bottom:	$30
	right:	$15	116	left:	$15
91	left:	$25		right:	$15
	right:	$250-350	117	left:	$12
		with box		right:	$15
92		$85	118	top:	$25
93	top:	$45 each		bottom:	$25
	bottom:	$40-55 each	119	top:	$20
94	top:	$225		bottom:	$45
	bottom:	$300-400	120	top:	$40
		with box		bottom:	$25
95	top:	$200 with	121	top:	$12

Page	Position	Price	Page	Position	Price
	bottom:	$50		bottom:	$10
122	top:	$5	126	top:	$20 each
	bottom:	$8		bottom:	$6
123	top:	$15	127	top:	$30 each
	bottom:	$5		bottom:	$15
124		$5-10 each	128	top:	$25
125	top:	$15-20		bottom:	$2-4